Dysgraphia

A Parent's Guide to Understanding Dysgraphia and Helping a Dysgraphic Child

by Nathan G. Brant

Table of Contents

Introduction 1

Chapter 1: Defining Dysgraphia & Identifying the 3 Types ..7

Chapter 2: Common Misconceptions about Dysgraphia 11

Chapter 3: Diagnosing Dysgraphia..15

Chapter 4: Disabilities Alongside Dysgraphia 19

Chapter 5: Treating Dysgraphia..23

Chapter 6: Dysgraphia and its Emotional Impact 27

Chapter 7: Working with Educators 31

Conclusion..33

Introduction

For a parent, the process of identifying and working with a child with a learning disability certainly can produce a decent amount of roadblocks. A key fact to recognize is that children are diagnosed with learning disorders and disabilities every day. And a 2012 NCLD (National Center for Learning Disabilities) survey indicated that there are almost two thousand adults living with learning disabilities as well. This study also showed that sixty-two percent of those surveyed say that the diagnosis of a learning disability involves team effort from both the child's parents and educators. It also showed that seventy-six percent of those surveyed understand learning disabilities to be diagnosed during the early school ages.

In many cases, parents go through stages of acceptance when it comes to acknowledging problems with their child's learning. Many parents ignore the potential signs of their child having a learning disability; it is not uncommon for any parent to be in denial of a problem. However, it is much more dangerous to ignore the signs rather than face them head on. It is important that parents are educated about their child's learning disability. The necessity is simply undeniable. The strain of overcoming a difficult hurdle in your child's life will take patience, understanding, discipline, and a high level of encouragement.

Approximately 5% of American public school students have identified learning disabilities; 42% of which receive accommodations for their learning disabilities. With these numbers, it is difficult for anyone to ignore the possibility that their child might have a learning disability. Two-thirds of those surveyed in the 2012 NCLD study stated they have no knowledge of dysgraphia. This can make it especially difficult to recognize and understand the signs. As a parent, you must work with your child and for your child to understand where there are issues and difficulties. This book will help you move forward in identifying and accommodating your child's learning needs.

Chapter 1: Defining Dysgraphia and Identifying the 3 Types of Dysgraphia

Dysgraphia is a learning disability that affects writing ability, fine motor skills, and information processing skills. The true definition of dysgraphia is "the inability to write coherently, as a symptom of brain disease or damage". This particular disability can manifest itself in a variety of ways in people of all ages. In all cases of dysgraphia, writing takes copious amounts of energy and focus. When speaking in terms of identifying dysgraphia, it is often classified as one of three types: dyslexic dysgraphia, motor dysgraphia, and spatial dysgraphia.

In cases of dyslexic dysgraphia, unplanned or spontaneous writing tasks are typically illegible and the spelling is very poor. However, copied notes, in this case, can be fairly easy to decipher. Understand that naming this type of dysgraphia as "dyslexic dysgraphia" is not automatically assuming or implying that your child also has dyslexia.

Motor dysgraphia varies greatly from dyslexic dysgraphia. Motor dysgraphia directly refers to the muscle capabilities of your child (fine motor skills, muscle tone, motor clumsiness, etc.) In cases such as this, your child's handwriting is likely illegible, even if the task is as simple as copying a set of notes or text. It can take your child an extensive amount of focus and time to accurately form complete letters and words in a short writing sample. Because of this, your child usually will not sustain the act of writing for very long. Writing is particularly difficult and physically uncomfortable for the motor dysgraphic child.

Spatial dysgraphia is what causes children to have the most illegible handwriting. In this particular case of dysgraphia, your child may not have a clear grasp on the concept of proper spacing, therefore resulting in compressed letters, words, sentences, or lack of clarity with concepts in general. Spelling is not usually an issue in this case, but there is still a chance that it could be an issue.

When dysgraphia presents itself in children, it produces difficulties in a variety of ways. It is important for every parent to know and understand most of the warning signs associated with dysgraphia. Some children can display symptoms from every aspect of dysgraphia. This is not uncommon, but it can prove to be particularly difficult to cater to your child's needs. If your child is experiencing difficulty in a multitude of areas, you should consider the options regarding assisted learning and additional training.

Chapter 2: Common Misconceptions about Dysgraphia

It is not unusual for people to be unfamiliar with facts about learning disabilities, particularly dysgraphia. Many people are only familiar with dyslexia, which is, in fact, one of the more common learning disabilities known. Of course, people also tend to create new ideas for what they believe to be true about learning disabilities such as dysgraphia.

To clear up the common misconceptions, here are some facts about dysgraphia that you should know:

Sloppy handwriting is not a sure-fire indicator of having Dysgraphia.

Multitudes of people are considered to have untidy – and occasionally undecipherable – handwriting. While illegible handwriting is often identified as the top indicator of dysgraphia, it is not the only factor when determining the presence of this learning disability. Signs such as muscle ache, lack of focus, and becoming extremely tired when writing are typically noticed alongside illegible handwriting before diagnosing a child with dysgraphia. It is important to identify the signs and symptoms and receive an official diagnosis from a medical professional before telling your child that they have dysgraphia or any other learning disability.

Dysgraphic children are not simply being lazy.

A child with dysgraphia often finds writing tasks terribly exhausting and frustrating. Some people cannot, or simply refuse to understand, the psychological ordeal with which these children are faced. Dysgraphic children focus intently on the writing tasks they are given, and put as much effort into them as they are able. Writing does not come easily to a child with dysgraphia, so it is important to acknowledge the effort they put forth instead of invalidating it.

Dysgraphia does not relate to a lack of intelligence.

People often associate poor focus and low motivation to being unintelligent. This is not always the case. Having a low IQ does not instantly result in having dysgraphia, or any other learning disability. The same applies in reverse: children with dysgraphia do not always have a low IQ. In fact, many children diagnosed with dysgraphia are often very bright children and participate in special programs at their schools.

Dysgraphia and Dyslexia are NOT the same thing.

The number of people who consider dysgraphia and dyslexia to be synonymous is incredible. The simultaneous appearance of these two learning disabilities is not uncommon, but this, unfortunately, brings confusion to some. Dyslexia is a reading disability, while dysgraphia is a writing disability. Both disabilities are recognized by a child's inability to properly recognize and process letters; this does not suggest that the two disabilities are anything more than related.

Dysgraphia is a lifelong condition without a "cure."

It is not unusual to find someone that believes children can simply "grow out of" dysgraphia. Unfortunately, dysgraphia is a condition that lasts a lifetime. Children that have dysgraphia carry it into adulthood. There is no cure or vaccine for dysgraphia. It is simply a challenge that people must live with and overcome in time. Of course, this is not to say that a child with dysgraphia cannot improve or succeed in writing. With the proper attention and with extra measures that are taken, a child can rise above their learning disability and carry that knowledge with them into adulthood.

After reading and understanding the facts to help clear up the common misconceptions, it is important for parents to share this information with others in their household. If parents can be aware of the true signs of dysgraphia, it will become easier for you to recognize the red flags in your own child's behavior and writing habits. Facing the struggle of dysgraphia is not an easy road for a child or a parent, which is why it is important that the facts are known so that children are not falsely diagnosed, harshly judged, or have their needs disregarded.

Chapter 3: Diagnosing Dysgraphia

Dysgraphia is not something that can immediately be determined from simply viewing a writing sample. A large number of people, particularly children, simply have sloppy handwriting, and do not have dysgraphia. To receive a diagnosis for dysgraphia, your child should visit a qualified clinician, physician, or licensed psychologist. These professionals have experience with identifying learning disabilities and can provide the appropriate tests. Alternate professions that can assist with diagnosing this are occupational therapists, school psychologists, and special educators.

The most common tests administered to those believed to have dysgraphia are IQ tests and self-generated writing samples. For example, an assessment may include age-appropriate text to be copied from the page, as well as a few self-generated sentences based on a particular topic. Assessments such as these are to be monitored. This way, a professional can properly evaluate the details that are not expressed on paper, such as physical strain, ability to focus, and other common symptoms of dysgraphia. These assessments are meant to accompany a professional's observations in order to properly diagnose any learning disabilities.

Problems that professionals look for when administering these tests can be categorized into six areas: attention, spatial ordering, sequential ordering, memory, higher-order cognition, and graphomotor. In terms of attention problems, this incorporates difficulties initiating, planning, and completing writing tasks. It can also represent immense fatigue from the act of writing. These traits are often identified from physical observation. Spatial and sequential ordering are often considered one in the same; both categories involve the proper organization of letters, words, sentences, and ideas on a page. Troubles in recalling prior knowledge that would typically be automatic for most are classified under memory problems. This prior knowledge to the writing process includes recalling spelling, using proper grammar, and simple punctuation rules. Higher-order cognition appears as a complicated term, but it is fairly simple. This term acknowledges the difficulty a child may have in bringing original thoughts and ideas to his or her writing. These issues generally arise in creative writing and critical thinking prompts, where on-the-spot content creation is necessary. Finally, professionals will assess graphomotor skills. Graphomotor skills involve the small finger muscles that allow for the proper gripping of writing utensils; this can prove incredibly difficult for a child with dysgraphia.

In many cases, for children who are especially exceptional, it can be difficult for people to identify a learning disability. If a child is particularly bright, people will usually assume the child is lazy or refuses to apply his or herself. In these cases, it is that much more important to pay attention to the signs, as your child's teachers could be missing the problem entirely.

Chapter 4: Disabilities Alongside Dysgraphia

While dysgraphia is a learning disability with its own unique qualities and symptoms, there are a number of cases in which it manifests itself alongside other learning disabilities. When this sort of situation arises, it is important for you as a parent to be aware of the symptoms and find ways to move forward.

Dysgraphia affects the fine motor skills and a child's ability to write; this is most closely associated with dyslexia. Like dysgraphia, dyslexia is regularly misunderstood. Dyslexia is an impaired reading disability that encompasses verbal fluency in reading, spelling abilities, and word decoding. It most commonly presents itself with impaired phonological coding, which is simply coding the sounds of spoken words into one's working memory. This is necessary in order to match spoken sounds to the corresponding letters of the alphabet. In having both dyslexia and dysgraphia, your child is more likely to have misspelled or incomplete words in their writing. They may also find it difficult planning the proper finger movements in sequence during tasks that involve keyboard processing.

Oral and written language disability (OWL LD) otherwise referred to as Selective Language Impairment (SLI), have also been noted to appear alongside dysgraphia. OWL LD (SLI) is a language disorder that creates problems with morphology, syntax, finding the right words, and making inferences beyond what is described in text. These disorders will typically affect speech, as well as written language. If these traits present themselves, they may present alongside the most common problems associated with dysgraphia.

ADHD is also commonly associated with dysgraphia. ADHD is the cause of intense distractions and inattentiveness during writing tasks. Children with ADHD often have problems sequencing information. They also produce thoughts at an extremely rapid rate, and often cannot physically keep up with their own thoughts. This, in combination with many other dysgraphic traits, is a situation could create a very difficult learning environment for your child.

Identifying the possibility of alternate learning disabilities in your child can assist you in realizing dysgraphia. Similarly, working towards treating these learning disabilities will most likely work for your child's benefit in overcoming his or her dysgraphia, as well.

Chapter 5: Treating Dysgraphia

While there is no documented treatment to eradicate dysgraphia, there are a wide range of coping strategies and steps that you as a parent can take to help your child get through the difficulties that come with this learning disability. There are three main steps involved with catering to dysgraphia: accommodation, modification, and remediation. Each strategy is equally important and should be considered when thinking of the progress of your child.

Accommodation involves providing your child with alternatives for written expression. One alternate method for writing is the use of Microsoft's word processor. It moves the process of written assignments along much more quickly without the stress or physical strain of forming letters and maintaining one script of writing.

Some children also find it useful to experiment with new writing tools; pencil grips can alleviate the pain of properly holding a pencil while writing.

Another simple alternative to written responses is to allow students to answer orally or via tape recorder. Visual projects and oral reports are common options available in many classes, where your child may excel without the use of extensive writing.

You can also recommend to your child's teachers to print out the notes given in class, as taking down notes as they are given can be a difficult process for a child with dysgraphia. Discuss with your child's teacher about the possibility of allowing more group projects and alternative method assignments, to better accommodate your child, as well as any other students that may have similar struggles.

Changing your expectations for your child's assignments is referred to as "modification". This strategy often includes allowing additional time for children to complete writing assignments. Creating milestones in an extensive assignment is also a useful and overlooked strategy. It is important that a child with dysgraphia does not feel rushed in the act of writing, seeing as how it can be a difficult process. Avoid chastising or ridiculing your child for sloppy or poorly written work; Praise them for the work they have accomplished and work with them to improve it if necessary. These are the types of skills parents and children can work together to achieve.

The word "remediation" can be explained as helping your child improve their writing skills and handwriting through giving specific instructions. Approaches such as muscle training and the over-teaching of good techniques are effective ways to remediate. Familiarization is often the best technical approach for overcoming dysgraphia. While you may utilize the accommodation of word processor for your child, it is still important that he or she understands how to produce legible handwriting. Take time out to focus on handwriting technique with your child (gripping the writing utensil, forming complete letters and words, consistency, etc.) If your child is having extreme difficulties handling their dysgraphia, it may be helpful to bring them to an occupational therapist or other special educator. These professionals have expertise in areas concerning learning disabilities, and can provide exceptional service for your child's learning.

It is very important that you are aware of the strategies that help dysgraphia. It is equally important that you share this with your child's educators. Helping a child with dysgraphia takes equal effort from both their parents as well as their teachers. Discussions with teachers on a regular basis can prove useful in acknowledging the progress your child is or is not making. These are the best steps you can take, on a technical level, to help your child conquer dysgraphia.

Chapter 6: Dysgraphia and its Emotional Impact

For a child with dysgraphia, there are not only physical disadvantages, but also emotional effects that come along, which are often disregarded. Having a learning disability will surely impact children's self-esteem, which, in turn, affects their work ethic and confidence levels. As a parent, it can be difficult to learn that your child has a learning disability, but it is your responsibility to make sure they don't let that information stop them from moving forward.

While struggling with dysgraphia, your child may experience difficulties socially. If your child is faced with complicated writing assignments, he or she can very easily become frustrated—to the point of regular temper tantrums. This can cause disruptions not only in the home, but in a school environment as well. Additionally, disabilities such as this can cause your child to lack the necessary social cues to progress in any social environment. The language processing difficulties associated with dysgraphia may make it hard for your child to understand certain nuances and sarcasms.

Dysgraphia has the potential to diminish your child's confidence level. If your child consistently falls short with writing assignments and classroom tasks, he or she will begin to think of his or herself as "bad" at school. With a sense of being different from other kids, it will often lower your child's self-esteem and overall applied effort in school. It is important for you as a parent to work with your child regularly and assure them that, even with their learning disability, they have the potential to excel in school.

Encouragement is key when it comes to overcoming a learning disability. Parents are the first influence a child has, which is why your acceptance and reassurance are crucial for your child's success.

Alternatively, some parents make the conscious decision to consult a professional about the effects dysgraphia has had on their child's emotional state. Taking your child to a psychologist or therapist is not uncommon. Many qualified professionals have experience dealing with emotional trauma as a result of the difficulties that stem from learning disorders. Working with therapists, your child could potentially show significant improvement.

Chapter 7: Working with Educators

While parents can feel overwhelmed by discovering that their child has dysgraphia, educators also experience difficulties in the classroom. As a parent, you should get involved with your child's school to ensure they are getting the absolute best learning experience that they possibly can.

It is important for you, the parent, to establish a strong working connection with your child's teachers. This creates a bridge of communication that will become extremely important as the school year passes. It is necessary for you to trust your child's teachers, and vice versa, otherwise no true work can be done. When speaking with your child's teachers, you should make your child's needs specific clear and communicate the manner in which you would like them addressed. Teachers are professionals in their field and often have useful suggestions in regards to accommodating your child's particular learning style.

As your child is given assignments, you can assess how they perform at home while the teacher does the same in the classroom. Frequent meetings, whether in person or over the phone, are very important because they provide an opportunity for you and the teacher to discuss concerns, as well as progress, in your child. Discuss how homework is performed and whatever difficulties your child may have had with it. Together, you and your child's teacher can determine the appropriate steps to encourage progress in dealing with and overcoming dysgraphia.

Conclusion

Parenting a child with a learning disability has its share of difficulties. While the process of identifying and acknowledging the learning disability is hard on both you and your child, discovering ways to overcome the challenge builds character and determination in your child. Recognizing the warning signs for dysgraphia is difficult for an uninformed parent, which is why it is important to know the facts about this disability and ways to overcome it. Working with educators to observe your child and where they are struggling is of the utmost importance in this regard.

It is important for every parent to accept the possibility of their child being diagnosed with a learning disability. Being aware of the symptoms and challenges associated with dysgraphia, along with other commonly occurring learning disabilities, is half of the battle. It is advisable for you, the parents, to learn and understand the warning signs involved when it comes to your child and his or her struggles within the learning environment. Because of the studies that have been conducted, the resources to tackle dysgraphia, as well as other learning disabilities, are readily available.

Ultimately, the true challenge lies in your ability to patiently help your child through his or her educational obstacles. As a parent, you should take it upon yourself to explore the assemblage of recommended strategies for coping with dysgraphia. Combined with therapy, emotional support, and in class techniques, strategies practiced at home will certainly show improvements in your child's writing abilities.

Finally, I'd like to thank you for purchasing this book! If you found it helpful, I'd greatly appreciate it if you'd take a moment to leave a review on Amazon. Thank you!